Weather

Weather

Have you ever
wondered why some
days start bright
and sunny, but end
in stormy showers?

Why do some days
begin with rain but
end in clear skies?

Why does the
weather change?

2

The weather changes because of the constant movement of air in the atmosphere.

These changes come in many forms such as wind, rain, or snow.

3

Air Masses

Air masses are enormous bodies of air with similar temperatures and moisture. Air masses move throughout the planet in different directions and at different speeds. They determine the temperature wherever they are located.

when a cold air mass and a warm air mass meet, this area is called a front. There are cold and warm fronts. An air mass that moves south from the North Pole will bring cold weather conditions. This is known as a cold air front, or a place where cold air replaces warm air. In a warm front, warm air replaces cold air. If a warm air mass over the ocean travels inland, it will bring warm and humid conditions.

Clouds

No matter what kind of weather, it is very likely you will see clouds in the sky. Clouds are accumulations of water or ice in the atmosphere. There are three types of clouds.

- Cirrus Clouds

Cirrus clouds look like thin white feathers floating in the air. They are the highest clouds in the sky. Because the temperatures at that elevation are very cold, cirrus clouds are usually made up of ice crystals.

- **Cumulus Clouds**

Cumulus clouds look like giant cotton balls in the sky. They are usually made up of water droplets, but if it is cold enough, the droplets will turn to ice crystals.

- Stratus Clouds

Stratus clouds are the closest to the ground. They look like a dark grey blanket covering the sky. Stratus clouds bring rain and storm showers.

Climate

Climate is different from weather. It is the average weather conditions found in one area over a long period of time. What makes the difference in climate is temperature.

Some places in the world are typically very cold and dry.

Others are rainy and foggy.

While other places are usually hot and humid.

Every part of the planet has a particular climate. Think about where you live? How is the climate in your hometown?

Climate Affects Our Lives

Climate on Earth is changing constantly. This is in part because of natural effects in the environment. However, humans are also responsible for the changes in climate. We produce different kinds of chemicals and gases that are released in the atmosphere and cause the Earth to get warmer.

Global warming has created adverse effects to our planet. For example, ice glaciers have started to melt, ocean waters have gotten warmer, and animals have suffered the consequences. Also, there have been more floods, tornadoes, and hurricanes. Fortunately, people around the world are taking steps to fix this problem. Here are some things you can do to help:

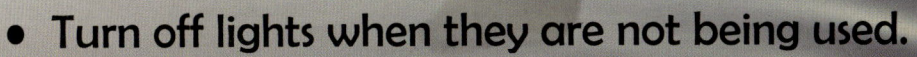

- Turn off lights when they are not being used.
- Ride a bike instead of a car.
- Minimize the heat or air conditioning when you are not at home.

Meteorologists

We cannot control the weather, but we can predict it. Meteorologists study past and present weather conditions to make forecasts about the weather.

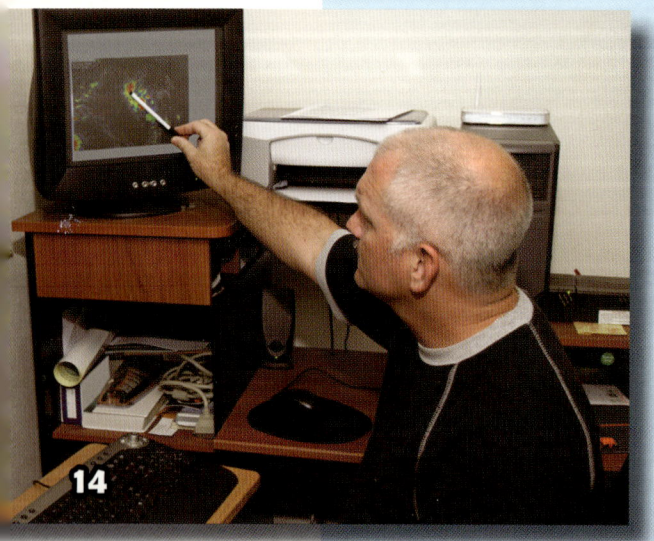

To help them do their job, meteorologists use satellites, airplanes, and computers. Would you like to be a meteorologist?

Being aware of the weather conditions can help you prepare for any changes headed your way.

You can find out if you need to carry an umbrella, wear shorts, or take a jacket to school. Do you know what the weather will be like tomorrow?

Atmosphere: air that surrounds the Earth.

Climate: kind of weather a place has over a long period of time.

Cloud: mass of water droplets or ice formed in the sky.

Forecast: to tell what is coming; to predict.

Global Warming: gradual increase in global temperatures caused by the release of gases that trap the sun's heat in the atmosphere.

Meteorologist: person who studies the atmosphere and weather conditions.

Precipitation: process by which water falls from the sky in form of rain, hail, sleet, or snow.